KĀMOHO THE CHAMELEON DOESN'T LIKE SCHOOL

Written by Kelly Gray Marrotte

Illustrated by Kelsie Kalohi

This story is based on real life occurrences of Derrick "Kutmaster Spaz" Kāmohoalii Bulatao. After encountering extreme bullying as a child and teen, Kutmaster Spaz dedicated his time visiting schools speaking to youth about his experience being bullied. This book is dedicated to his former teacher, Ms. Watase of Kapunahala Elementary School. With her patience and guidance, Spaz learned he was smart and he could do anything he put his mind to. Mahalo Ms. Watase and all of the teachers out there making a difference every day!

KĀMOHO THE CHAMELEON DOESN'T LIKE SCHOOL by Kelly Gray Marrotte

Published by Kelly Gray Marrotte
5090 Likini Street PH202
Honolulu, HI 968189

Cover and Illustrations by Kelsie Kalohi

Story based on real life occurrences of Derrick "Kutmaster Spaz" Bulatao

ISBN: 978-1-7375768-1-5

Printed in United States

It was a beautiful sunny day and Kāmoho's alarm was ringing to wake him up for school.

"Ughhhh, I don't want to go to school," said Kāmoho.
Kāmoho was so upset, he threw his covers down as he sat up.

"Why do I have to go to school?" complained Kāmoho.

"School is so hard," Kāmoho sighed as he ate his breakfast.

"I can't read."

"I can't write."

"I can't add."

"School is only for smart kids!"

Just as Kāmoho got to school the morning bell rang.

Kāmoho got to class just in time.
"Good Morning Kāmoho!" said Ms. Watase.

"Good Morning," mumbled Kāmoho, not looking happy at all to be there.

"Everyone will take turns reading out loud today," said Ms. Watase.

Kāmoho didn't like reading out loud for everyone to hear.

He made mistakes and sometimes stuttered. He felt the other kids would laugh at him.

Kāmoho raised his hand and asked if he could go to the health room.

Ms.Watase shook
her head no.

"You will be okay
Kāmoho," she said.
"We will do it
together!"

Kāmoho was really feeling sick. He always got a stomach ache when he had to read out loud.

When it was Kāmoho's turn, Ms. Watase came and sat next to him by his desk.

Kāmoho began to read. "The ffffrog and ttoad hopppp..."

Ms. Watase used her finger
to guide Kāmoho under
a word.

She gently encouraged him while smiling at him as he continued to read.

Kāmoho finished the sentence and Ms.Watase clapped her hands in excitement.

"You did it Kāmoho!" Ms. Watase exclaimed.
"I am so proud of you."

Ms. Watase explained to the class. "Sometimes school work is hard but we must keep trying."

"I know each and every one of you can do the work," said Ms. Watase. "I believe in you," she said as she looked at Kāmoho.

Kāmoho felt good. He did it. He read out loud with Ms. Watase's help and she was proud of him.

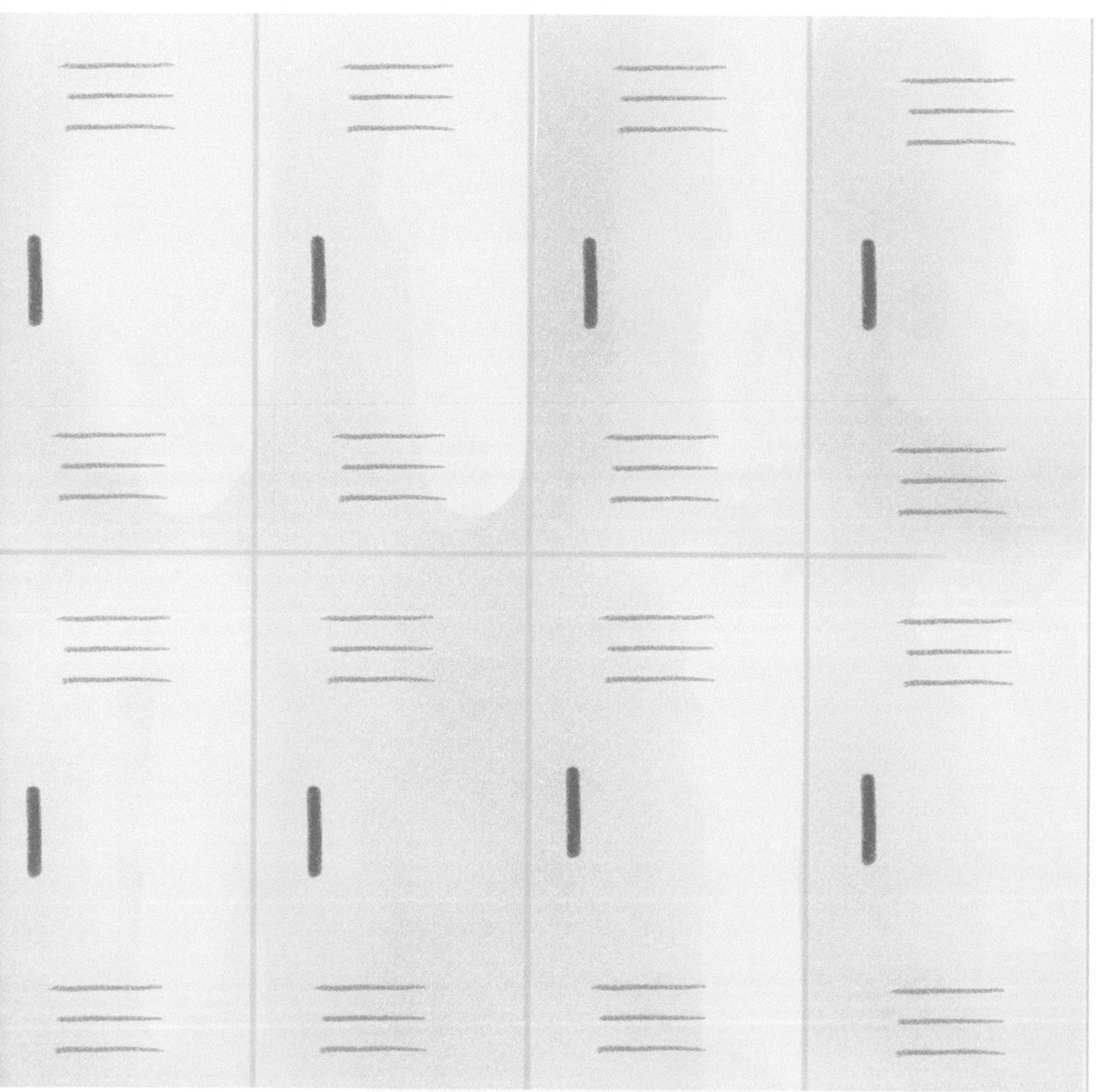

I DID IT!

"I do like school and I can read!" Kāmoho thought on his walk home from school.

"Ms. Watase said she believes in me, so I will believe in myself too!" Kāmoho shouted happily.

KĀMOHO'S LIFE LESSON

In this story, Kāmoho learned that even though he had a hard time reading he could do it. He just needed someone to believe in him so he could believe in himself.

If you find yourself struggling, all you have to do is remember that I believe in you!

www.ingramcontent.com/pod-product-compliance
Ingram Content Group UK Ltd.
Pitfield, Milton Keynes, MK11 3LW, UK
UKHW060117300726
14090UKWH00002B/237

* 9 7 8 1 7 3 7 5 7 6 8 1 5 *